Financial Dominion

How To Take Charge
of Your Finances

Financial Dominion

How To Take Charge of Your Finances

by
Norvel Hayes

Harrison House
Tulsa, Oklahoma

Unless otherwise indicated, all Scripture quotations are taken from the *King James Version* of the Bible.

3rd Printing
Over 21,000 in Print

Financial Dominion
How To Take Charge of Your Finances
ISBN 0-89274-703-X
Copyright © 1986 by Norvel Hayes
P. O. Box 1379
Cleveland, Tennessee 37311
(Formerly *Prosperity Now,* ISBN 0-89274-416-2)

Published by Harrison House, Inc.
P. O. Box 35035
Tulsa, Oklahoma 74153

. . . as long as he sought the Lord, God made him to prosper.

2 Chronicles 26:5

Save now, I beseech thee, O Lord: O Lord, I beseech thee, send now prosperity.

Psalm 118:25

Contents

INTRODUCTION

It is my intention to help the reader to understand the purpose and plan of God's will in the area of prosperity, success, and victory. In this book, I will share the truths from the Bible that God has revealed to me by His Spirit and through more than 20 years of experience in the ministry.

God desires for every one of His children to experience victory, success, and prosperity in every area of life. He wants to bless you even more than you want to be blessed. The problem is that most Christians are not in a position for these blessings to be manifested. Most of them may experience some minor blessings, but the great blessings that God has prepared for them may never reach them.

That problem is why the Lord instructed me to write this book and to share with the Body the things God has taught me, as well as how I came into a position where I could be mightily blessed of God. When you learn these principles and how to apply them in everyday life, you are in position for the abundant life that Jesus came to give all of us.

In Psalm 35:27, God said that He has pleasure in the prosperity of His servant. As we shall see in the up and coming chapters, the prosperity of the servant of God is given for only one reason — so that the servant may prosper *in his service to God.*

If I can convince you to believe what God Almighty said and can get you to do what He told us to do, you will receive blessings, victory, and joy beyond what you could ask or think.

> . . . Believe in the Lord your God, so shall ye be established; believe his prophets, so shall ye prosper.
>
> 2 Chronicles 20:20

1
SEEK GOD AND PROSPER

If I can convince you to seek the Lord, you will be able to prosper in any area of your life. The reason most people are not prospering in some areas of their lives is because they are not seeking the Lord in those areas. As long as anyone seeks the Lord, He will make him to prosper. James 1:17 says:

> Every good gift and every perfect gift is from above, and cometh down from the Father of lights, with whom is no variableness, neither shadow of turning.

Good Things Come From Heaven

You must understand that good gifts and perfect gifts come down from Heaven for you. Not one defeated, beaten down, confused day has ever come down from Heaven. Heaven has no defeat. Heaven has no confusion. Heaven has no sickness or disease. Everything we receive from Heaven is good and perfect.

The devil is the one who puts all kinds of sickness and disease on people, but the reason he can do that is because they have not spent enough quality time seeking Jesus the Healer. As long as you spend time entirely devoted to seeking Jesus as healer, God Almighty will show you how to be healed and how to enjoy good health.

The Abundant Life

The Lord Jesus Christ, the Son of the living God, has paid the price for us to live and have our being in abundant life. The Bible says that living without God's blessing and prosperity is like living in the dust.

God has only prepared one kind of life for us, and that is the abundant life. If you are living in a beaten down, sick, defeated, half-poverty, wonder-where-the-rent's-coming-from life, that is not the kind of life God has prepared for you. In John 10:10 the Lord Jesus says:

> **The thief cometh not, but for to steal, and to kill, and to destroy: I am come that they might have life, and that they might have it more abundantly.**

If you have seen the news on television or read the newspaper lately, you know there are two things that pervade the lives of most people. Those things are poverty and bad health. Poverty, sickness, and disease plague the world continually. They are part of the devil's way of attempting to destroy God's creation, but they come on man through God's law of sin and death. The law of the Spirit of life in Christ Jesus, thank God, has made us free from the law of sin and death. Those who have Christ do not have to be affected by the law of sin and death.

> **For the law of the Spirit of life in Christ Jesus hath made me free from the law of sin and death.**
>
> **Romans 8:2**

If you seek the Lord Jesus and operate in the laws of the Spirit that bring life and health, you will prosper and be in health even as your soul prospers. (3 John 2.) The area of your life in which you seek the Lord is the area in which He will cause you to prosper. It does not make any difference which phase or area of your life this is — finances, health, family or social relationships, business or investments. Whatever area in which you seek Him, you will find Him.

The usual reason most people have not found God in financial prosperity is because they have not been seeking enough in that area. The most common reason they have not found God in the area of health and divine healing is because they have not put in enough quality time seeking Jesus as healer. Anyone who studies the Bible and seeks Jesus as healer can find Him.

How to Seek God

It amazes me to find out that people attending many churches that call themselves "Bible-believing" find there is no one in the church who can help them when they get attacked by the devil. Also, when they get backed up against the wall in some area of their lives, they do not have the knowledge of how to obtain anything from God for themselves.

This is what happened to me when my daughter developed growths on her body. For five years, I prayed for her, but she did not receive healing. Finally, I became so tired of praying and not getting my prayers answered that I decided to seek God until I knew what the problem was. If it was possible to find out the truth about this situation from God, I determined to pay the price. I was not going to have my daughter running around with those horrible growths on her body for the rest of her life.

A doctor cut the growths off — and they just grew back and brought all their cousins with them! After all of that, I began to seek God for myself.

I got down on my knees and cried out to God. I said, "God, I am seeking You as a healer. Jesus, I am seeking for You to come to my house as the same healer You were in the first chapter of the Book of Mark. Jesus, I read in that chapter about a man who had leprosy and sneaked away from the camp where he was isolated to seek You for healing.

"So, Jesus, today I am sneaking out from my own way of thinking, from the 'religious' church world, from casual praying, from men's doctrines that say You only ask God once and never bring it up again, and from everything else I have tried that has not worked. I am sneaking away, God, and I am going to seek You until Heaven falls to earth. I am seeking the Jesus I see in the first chapter of Mark. Just as that leper kept on seeking and looking for You, so I am going to keep on looking and seeking for You until I find You. No matter how long I look and seek, I will not stop until I come face to face with You."

If you want to hear from Heaven, why don't you start thinking the way Matthew, Mark, Luke, and John thought, instead of trying to figure out everything for yourself or according to the way your friends believe? Your friends are like my friends, they don't have the power. *Only God has the power!* God did not tell us to seek our friends; He told us to seek Him.

I told God that I wanted to know the truth and that I would not stop asking Him until I received the truth. It was not very long before God showed me the answer. He showed me supernaturally how to get the growths off my daughter's body.

Diligence

You must see to it that you seek the Lord diligently with all your heart. You cannot be a casual Christian who attends church on Sunday, sings a few songs, says a short prayer, and hope that something good will happen to you. If you are not sure and really don't know — maybe it will, maybe it won't; but you're wondering if God will bless you — then you will continue to wonder.

In God, there is no "wondering." You either know or you don't know, and there is *no in-between!* You either know that Jesus is your healer, or you don't know. You either believe it, or you don't believe it. Wondering is always doubt, and doubt means disbelief.

Most people live in the "world of wondering" — wondering what in the world will happen tomorrow: Will God ever heal me? Can I ever be free from sickness and disease or free from these twisted, crooked legs, or from these blind eyes? Will I ever be able to pay my bills and get free from poverty and lack? Is there any hope for me?

As long as you're wondering about it, there will never be any hope for you. God does not work through wondering. God works through believing. Wondering is doubt, and doubt, as the 14th chapter of Romans says, is sin. The Bible says that sin separates man from God. Any area where you allow doubt will be plagued with the curses of the world for the rest of your life.

> But let him ask in faith, nothing wavering. For he that wavereth is like a wave of the sea driven with the wind and tossed.
>
> For let not that man think that he shall receive any thing of the Lord.
>
> A double minded man is unstable in all his ways.
>
> **James 1:6-8**

The man who doubts God won't receive anything from the Lord, so he shouldn't even *think* that he will receive. If he doubts, he is *not* going to receive.

Now that we are living under the New Covenant, all we need to go before God is faith in Him. If you've got the faith in God, He loves you so much that He will manifest Himself. When you seek the Lord, He will cause you to prosper in every phase of your life, including finances. Don't put finances off to one side and think He won't bless you in that area. I know that He will because He promised to do that. He desires for His children to prosper in every area of their lives.

Beloved, I wish above all things that thou mayest prosper and be in health, even as thy soul prospereth.

3 John 2

Make Up Your Mind

It is just as easy to decide to believe God and His Word as it is to decide to keep on wondering. If you're sick and dying, you may be just one decision away from your healing. You must make up your mind to believe.

You may say, "Brother Norvel, that's not as easy as you say, because I grew up in a certain kind of church." But it *is* just as easy — if you make your mind up to ask God to deliver you from a carnal way of thinking and from the doctrines and traditions of men. Ask God to put His mind inside you, the mind of Christ, the mind of Matthew, Mark, Luke, and John.

Some people ask me if they have to accept some truth that God has for them. I have news for them! They have gotten all they are going to get from God if their spirits and minds basically remain closed to spiritual things. Being closed to spiritual truth is what keeps people in a "world of wondering."

If you allow Jesus to become your healer, then you can receive healing. Whatever you seek God for, and *allow* Jesus to become to you, that's what He will become to you. God's knowledge and power must be allowed to operate on the inside of you, down in your spirit, and in your mind.

> **But without faith it is impossible to please him: for he that cometh to God must believe that he is, and that he is a rewarder of them that diligently seek him.**
>
> **Hebrews 11:6**
>
> **The young lions do lack, and suffer hunger: but they that seek the Lord shall not want any good thing.**
>
> **Psalm 34:10**

Many people are ashamed to call on Jesus and make Him their healer or their provider or whatever they are in need of that has been promised to them by God. They are afraid of what their friends or family will say about them. But if you stand there and call upon the Lord until you know that you know, you won't have this kind of shame at all. When you do seek the Lord, remember this: You only get from Him what you ask.

Many people seek God in vague or general terms and don't ask for specific things. If you need a miracle from Him, you need to seek Him as your own miracle worker. Those who seek God diligently will find Him.

You Are God's Beloved

You are not some kind of oddball, not knowing where you came from or who made you or for what purpose you are on earth. You are God's beloved, and He doesn't want you to be someone else. He wants you to be you! Don't envy anyone else. Find out why God made you, and find out your purpose. Of course, you'll never find that out unless you spend some quality time seeking Him. As long as you diligently seek the Lord, He will make you to prosper.

In 3 John 2, the Holy Spirit said through the apostle that He wants us, above all things, to prosper. If you continue attending a dried-up, sick church, however, you may never be rich. There are three things God hates: sin, poverty, and sickness. So if God hates it, what are you doing with it? Why not run those things out of your life? You will not get rid of poverty and sickness as long as you are content to live in them. If you seek the Lord, He can cause you to prosper in these areas.

Understand once and for all that Jesus is your personal healer, and you'll be on your way to health and victory. You need to learn what causes victory to come into your life. The things of God work without hindrance when you seek Him.

I learned years ago, through hearing other people's testimonies, the value of making Jesus my business partner. I walked the floor calling Jesus the best businessman I ever met, thanking Him for giving me wisdom and understanding and never letting me invest money in a place where I could lose it. I didn't become a multimillionaire by being stupid or by being smart. I became one because I sought the Lord with all my heart, mind, and strength, and God gave me prosperity.

Trust in the Lord with all thine heart; and lean not unto thine own understanding.

In all thy ways acknowledge him, and he shall direct thy paths.

Proverbs 3:5,6

2

IT PLEASES GOD TO GIVE YOU THE KINGDOM

But rather seek ye the kingdom of God; and all these things shall be added unto you.

Fear not, little flock; for it is your Father's good pleasure to give you the kingdom.

Luke 12:31,32

There has never been a nation on the face of the earth where people starved to death who sought and worshiped Christ. No human being who will worship Jesus needs to ever starve or go without clothes. Haven't you read that . . . **If then God so clothe the grass, which is to day in the field, and to morrow is cast into the oven; how much more will he clothe you, O ye of little faith** (Luke 12:28)?

Little faith will get you little blessings. No faith will get you no blessings, and great faith will get you great blessings. That means you need to trust God for everything and just boldly step out and believe Him. Be like Moses, who stretched out his hand and God parted the Red Sea for the Israelites to cross. That is just an example for you so that, when you stretch your hand up to God and show Him faith, then God's power will come to you for your need, whatever it is.

Jesus Our Alpha and Omega

Jesus is the alpha and omega of your life. He is the beginning and the ending, and He had better be *everything* from the beginning of your life to its ending, if you want to be prosperous. Unless you make Jesus your everything, from first to last in your life, then you are going to have a lot of pitfalls, battles, and mountains to climb throughout your days.

If you will make Jesus and the Word of God the height of your intelligence and life from beginning to end, you will avoid an awful lot of trouble in your life. Jesus is the only One who knows all about life. We only know in part and see through a glass darkly. (1 Cor. 13:12.) But Jesus doesn't operate in part. He operates in full. He has the Spirit without measure, but we have the Spirit *with* measure.

Having God prosper you does not mean just in the financial realm but in every area of your life. If you have cancer or some other disease and you begin to seek Jesus the Healer, you will find prosperity in the physical realm.

Take No Thought

Therefore take no thought, saying, What shall we eat? or, What shall we drink? or, Wherewithal shall we be clothed?

(For after all these things do the Gentiles seek:) for your heavenly Father knoweth that ye have need of all these things.

Matthew 6:31,32

Jesus doesn't want you to take any thought for your own prosperity. What do the Gentiles seek after? They seek after food, drink, and clothing. It's wrong when you start seeking those things, because you are not seeking first things first. God knows that you have need of food, drink, and clothes in your house and for your family, but God wants to be your provider and have you trust Him for all these things and not your own ability or strength.

> **But seek ye first the kingdom of God, and his righteousness; and all these things shall be added unto you.**
>
> Matthew 6:33

Jesus said that God's power will add all these things to you. If you seek the purposes and plans of God's kingdom and your right standing in the kingdom, prosperity automatically will come to you. If you are not going to God but trying to get these things the world's way, then God considers you an idolator because things and the world are being placed before Him. You are not putting Him first. When the Israelites operated that way in the Old Testament, God called the nations of Israel and Judah prostitutes. (Ezek. 23.)

If you ever stop seeking the Lord for your life and the things that you need, you will stop being prosperous and the devil will come in to ruin and destroy you eventually. But, if you make Jesus your life partner, you will have success.

God has nothing in His mind except being prosperous and successful. He is the height of prosperity and success. He has no defeat in His mind. He doesn't even think about poverty or not having enough. He doesn't even think about your children backsliding or your business not being successful, because He thinks successful all the time. It is His nature. If you will seek God first, He'll throw success and victory on you in every area of your life. It doesn't make any difference what it is as long as you're seeking Him first and are not involved in idolatry or whoremongering.

If you will take Jesus as your business partner and give God some of the profits from that business, it will begin to grow and grow. It will be so easy to run that business. Then, as you're faithful to seek the Lord first in that business, you will get another one. If you're faithful to put God first in the second one, He will give you still another and another. It will be no struggle at all when you turn things over to the Spirit of God because *your struggle ends when His Spirit begins.*

Humble yourselves therefore under the mighty hand of God, that he may exalt you in due time:

Casting all your care upon him; for he careth for you.

1 Peter 5:6,7

That is the way I had to learn everything, just cast all my care on Him and seek Him for the truth. I was just floating along through life not knowing very much about God, making $4,000 to $5,000 a week. All of a sudden — one night in my car — God came to me and wanted me to give Him my life. So I gave Him my life, or so I thought. But I couldn't turn loose of my businesses and corporations. I was a slave to them. I had been doing it so long and so successfully for so many years that I was in total bondage to them. Many businessmen are total slaves to their businesses. The little empire they are building isn't worth a thing, because they're in bondage to it.

Although I gave my life to Jesus, I was in such bondage to my businesses that I didn't know what to do. So I began to seek the Lord to get out of bondage.

I would pray and seek God for hours all alone, and the Lord would come to visit me three or four times a week. You see I couldn't jerk myself out of that bondage of wanting to make money and wanting to be successful.

Something continually possessed my mind and drove me to want to make another million or own another business. I couldn't get my thinking on things that would help and bless other people. All I could do was think about things that could help me and put more money in my bank accounts. Helping people was not my lifestyle, making money was. But Jesus wanted to change me.

> No man can serve two masters: for either he will hate the one, and love the other; or else he will hold to the one, and despise the other. Ye cannot serve God and mammon.
>
> Therefore I say unto you, Take no thought for your life, what ye shall eat, or what ye shall drink; nor yet for your body, what ye shall put on. Is not the life more than meat, and the body than raiment?
>
> Behold the fowls of the air: for they sow not, neither do they reap, nor gather into barns; yet your heavenly Father feedeth them. Are ye not much better than they?
>
> Which of you by taking thought can add one cubit unto his stature?
>
> And why take ye thought for raiment? Consider the lilies of the field, how they grow; they toil not, neither do they spin:
>
> And yet I say unto you, That even Solomon in all his glory was not arrayed like one of these.
>
> Wherefore, if God so clothe the grass of the field, which to day is, and to morrow is cast into the oven, shall he not much more clothe you, O ye of little faith?
>
> **Matthew 6:24-30**

God Gave Me a Supernatural Vision

God knows exactly what you need to get out of bondage and on the road to freedom. God knew what I needed. I was seeking God for total freedom, and I got it sitting on my bed one afternoon reading my Bible.

All of a sudden, the Spirit of God came on me and the whole room disappeared. I saw into another world. I saw a whole field of lilies, so peaceful and contented and beautiful. Then I came out of my body and went up in the air from where I was looking down, and into the field full of lilies. God pointed out a single lily and how beautiful it was because He had made it.

As I was looking at that beautiful lily, all of a sudden the scene changed, and I saw a big high-backed chair. It was a king's chair, but it was empty — just as your chair will be empty some day. Man is like a flower. He is alive for today, but one day he'll be cut down and be no more. If you are ever going to do anything for God and His kingdom, please start doing it now, because no one ever knows how much time he has left on this earth.

> **. . . it is appointed unto men once to die, but after this the judgment.**
>
> **Hebrews 9:27**

This king's chair that I saw was set on top of billions of dollars worth of gold. But the gold was all covered with green canker and mold. It was the ugliest mess I had ever seen in my life because the chair was empty and had no life in it. God had me take a long hard look at it. Then I came back to myself sitting on the bed, reading my Bible. The Lord spoke to me and said, "You just received a Bible vision. Look down."

When I looked down, I saw this verse: . . . **Why take ye thought for raiment?** (v. 28).

Then God said to me, "Why do you take thought for things that you need? If you seek Me, I will give them to you. Why don't you consider the lilies of the field and how they grow. They toil not, neither do they spin, and yet I say unto you that even Solomon in all his glory was not arrayed like one of them."

Solomon was the richest man who ever lived on earth, and also was a king, the highest position on earth. After I had that vision, I was set free from the bondage of making money just for myself. My entire being was set free totally. From then on, I began to see the true value of things on earth. I began doing such things as feeding the poor, passing out tracts, and working with high school kids to get them off drugs. I began to work in the ministry of helps as hard as I could. For seven years, I worked in the things of God with absolutely no pay and no offerings. So you can seek the Lord and prosper, but you will have to be willing to help others.

Today, whenever I get up to speak to an audience of several thousand people, the Lord often will remind me of the tracts I passed out and the high school kids I helped. He says, "Son, I'll never forget your faithfulness to Me in the city dump. Learn to bloom where you are planted."

After seven years in the ministry of helps, God told me one day that He wanted me to study the Bible on the subject of *faith*. He wanted me to start teaching His Word and everything that He had taught me. Now I have thousands of invitations to speak and teach the

Bible all over the world. It pays to be faithful and obedient to His Spirit.

3
OBEDIENCE BRINGS BLESSING

If ye be *willing* and *obedient*, ye shall eat the good of the land.

Isaiah 1:19

Unless you are *willing* to *obey* God and to *submit* to the Lordship of Jesus Christ, you may never receive very much in the way of prosperity or blessings at all. What most people haven't realized is that along with the promises and blessings of God comes the responsibility to use those blessings to help other people and to promote the gospel.

God will not bless selfishness, and He will not bless laziness. But if you show God that you are willing to share, witness and give — to lay your things at the apostles' feet (Acts 2:44-47) — then the blessings of Heaven will simply fall on you.

He openeth also their ear to discipline, and commandeth that they return from iniquity.

If they obey and serve him, they shall spend their days in prosperity, and their years in pleasures.

But if they obey not, they shall perish by the sword, and they shall die without knowledge.

Job 36:10-12

Steps to Promotion

One of the greatest gifts that God has given to the Church is the ministry of helps. God has set the ministry of helps in the Church just as He set the pastor and teacher in the Church.

> **And God hath *set* some in the church, first apostles, secondarily prophets, thirdly teachers, after that miracles, then gifts of healings, *helps*, governments, diversities of tongues.**
>
> **1 Corinthians 12:28**

Pastors are set as the shepherds over the churches. A pastor keeps the flock from scattering and keeps them working together.

Apostles do missionary work and travel to different areas starting churches. They also are administrators in church government and church doctrine. They are "sent ones" and, therefore, are sent out from a local church body.

Prophets need to share supernatural revelation knowledge with the local church. They are to prophesy by the Spirit of God about things that are happening now and things that are to come. A local church will never amount to very much in the supernatural realm without the ministry of the prophet in the church.

Every church needs to hear from teachers set in the Body as a whole with instruction in the Word of God. Local teachers also are very important, to give instruction continuously through the week and through the year. The teacher should set up special courses on a particular subject such as the Holy Spirit or the life of Jesus and teach it one night each week.

> **And he gave some, apostles; and some, prophets; and some, evangelists; and some, pastors and teachers;**

For the perfecting of the saints, for the work of the ministry, for the edifying of the body of Christ.

Ephesians 4:11,12

The local church body needs the fivefold ministry to prosper and come into the full maturity of the measure of the stature of Christ. The fivefold ministry is the hand of Jesus reaching out to His Body in order to perfect and edify them.

Ministry of Helps

If you have any questions as to what your particular area of ministry is or how to serve God, and if you don't know what you should do to get the blessing of God to flow in your life, then I will tell you. Start off by working in the ministry of helps. No matter what position you're in or what gifts God has given you, you'll always be working in the ministry of helps. Many ministers stop working in the ministry of helps when they start becoming popular.

I never intend to get out of the ministry of helps. If you ever stop helping people, you've had it. You will go through a dry and thirsty land where there is no water. If you ever go through a dry spell in your life where there never seems to be enough, start feeding the poor. Read the scriptures in the Bible on feeding the poor, and then *obey* them.

Jesus said that you can't even give someone a cup of cold water in His name without receiving a reward for it. Imagine what the Lord would do for you if you gave someone a cheeseburger or a steak. When you begin helping families that need help, it is then that the blessing of the Lord will really fall on you and return to you as you have given.

Pure religion and undefiled before God and the Father is this, To visit the fatherless and widows in their affliction, and to keep himself unspotted from the world.

James 1:27

But love ye your enemies, and do good, and lend, hoping for nothing again; and your *reward shall be great,* and ye shall be the children of the Highest: for he is kind unto the unthankful and to the evil.

Be ye therefore merciful, as your Father also is merciful.

Give, and it shall be given unto you; good measure, pressed down, and shaken together, and running over, shall men give into your bosom. For with the same measure that ye mete withal (give) it shall be measured to you again.

Luke 6:35,36,38

God will give you special gifts and rewards if you're willing to help people and work in the ministry of helps. But if you never help anybody, there will come a day when you'll wonder, "God, where are you?" God gives gifts to people who will obey His voice and are willing to serve Him with what He gives them and not just do their own thing all the time.

One of the gifts that God will give you is praying in other tongues. If you will spend some time during the day praying in other tongues, you'll come alive and receive power from on high.

But ye, beloved, building up yourselves on your most holy faith, praying in the Holy Ghost.

Jude 20

If you will be faithful to do this, then the gospel will never get old to you. Spend time in prayer and get out there and help people, and the gospel will never get old to you. Make sure you're always helping someone. Help who? People who need your help. It shouldn't matter who they are. If they need help, help them! If you do that willingly and continue to obey the gospel, God will make you rich and shower you with blessings.

There is always a need for volunteer help in homes for abused children or unwed mothers. Your prayers, wisdom, knowledge and funds can always be put to good use to bless others.

Receiving God's Gifts

It is very important to receive the gifts which God gives to the Church and to those in it. After I was in the ministry, the Lord began to use me in the area of prophecy. There were times, however, when I didn't want to prophesy. My heart would begin to hurt; but, when I obeyed the Lord, the pain would leave me. (God help us to obey the Holy Spirit.)

After I was obedient to the Lord for two or three years in this area, He began to give me a special anointing for speaking with other tongues. There are times when the Lord will send me somewhere to a meeting or a convention just to give a message in tongues. Just because you have the ministry of a gift from God doesn't mean that you can make it work anytime you want. It is only as the Spirit wills.

When God asks you to work in the ministry of helps, you should volunteer to do so. If you refuse, that may be as far as you'll ever get with God. You may end up living in a spiritually dry land for the rest of your life. You could live and die and never get where God wants you to be. If God can't trust you to work in a ministry where all you do is give without getting anything in return, then He can't trust you with the riches of Heaven.

For seven years, I contributed money to the ministry of helps. I bought the food and fed the poor myself. I didn't want any offerings. I was doing it because the Lord wanted me to do it. (He wants you to bless others also.) He blessed me so much with the blessings of Heaven that I wasn't even looking for any money. I was so thrilled that I could just be involved in the work of God and be in His presence that money wasn't important. If money ever does become so important to a person that it is the reason he does God's work, he is in danger of falling away from God and into total destruction. (Do things for Jesus because you love Him.)

> **But godliness with contentment is great gain.**
>
> **For we brought nothing into this world, and it is certain that we can carry nothing out.**
>
> **And having food and raiment let us be therewith content.**
>
> **But *they that will be rich* fall into temptation and a snare, and into many foolish and hurtful lusts, which drown men in *destruction* and perdition.**
>
> **For the *love* of money is the *root* of all evil: which while some coveted after, they have erred from the faith, and pierced themselves through with many sorrows.**
>
> **1 Timothy 6:6-10**

If there is one thing that marks the present generation of people, it is their will or desire to be rich and famous (successful). Ask yourself why you are serving the Lord. Is it because of His gifts and blessings that He has promised you? Do you love God's *presents* more than you love His *presence?* Many people love Him just because of Who He is. Love the gifts *more* than the Giver.

This way of thinking is totally opposed to the laws that operate in the Kingdom of God. If one continues to think and believe along these lines, he is headed for deception and "many sorrows." The only way to receive the things you want from God is to give Him what He wants from you.

> Jesus said unto him, If thou wilt be perfect, go and sell that thou hast, and give to the poor, and thou shalt have treasure in heaven: and come and follow me.
>
> But when the young man heard that saying, he went away *sorrowful*: for he had great possessions.
>
> Matthew 19:21,22
>
> Then said Jesus unto his *disciples*, if any man will come after me, let him *deny himself*, and take up his cross, and follow me.
>
> For whosoever will save his life shall lose it: and whosoever will lose his life for my sake shall find it.
>
> For what is a man profited, if he shall gain the whole world, and lose his own soul? or what shall a man give in exchange for his soul?
>
> Matthew 16:24-26

Show God That He Can Trust You

I got so tired of driving expensive cars and having so much money and not being close to God or knowing if I was going to Heaven or not. I got so tired of living in a dry and thirsty wasteland. When I got in the presence of God, I saw how good and tender He was and how much He loved me. Then I began to see those things in the right perspective and to realize that the Bible is true. When I began to see how the Word works, I started to obey God and do anything He asked me to do.

You need to *show* God that He can trust you and that you'll do what He asks you to do. God doesn't just want to hear what you'll do for Him. He wants to see what you'll do and if you will obey Him when He asks you to do something. Always remember this: God doesn't bless lazy people or stingy people. You must be free with your financial giving, with your time, and with your life. Spend your time doing things for God. Spend some of your time working in the ministry of helps.

> **What doth it profit, my brethren, though a man say he hath *faith*, and have not works? can faith save him?**
>
> **If a brother or sister be naked, and destitute of daily food,**
>
> **And one of you say unto them, Depart in peace, be ye warmed and filled; notwithstanding ye give them not those things which are needful to the body; what doth it profit?**
>
> **Even so faith, if it hath not works, is *dead*, being alone.**
>
> **Yea, a man may say, Thou hast faith, and I have works: *shew* me thy faith without thy works, and I will *shew* thee my faith by my works.**
>
> **James 2:14-18**

Faith without works is dead! Totally dead! You could memorize the entire Book of Hebrews, but sit home and watch television, and you would be the same spiritually as a walking dead man. But if you get out there and help others, then the life of God will come to you.

There are two things that you can't give away to God: your money and your life. The more of your life that you give away to God, the more of His life will come to you. The more faithful you are to use and give your money to God and His work, the more He showers His blessings upon you. After a few years of faithful service to the Lord (God will watch you for a while to test your faithfulness), then He will begin to open up the windows of Heaven and pour out on you what is known as "overtaking blessings."

You can find tremendous favor with God by making one simple decision. Make up your mind to go to work helping people so that God can reward you. Don't let your life go by without helping those who are going hungry or without clothes or shelter. Remember, God doesn't bless lazy or stingy people.

One night about 12 years ago, I was in Carbondale, Illinois, on my way to speak at a meeting. While I was sitting in the car, my heart began to hurt so badly I could hardly stand it. It continued to hurt while I walked up on the platform. I didn't know if I was going to be able to speak. But when I got up to speak, the Lord spoke to me and told me to call down to the front everyone who had a bad heart. The Lord said He was going to give everyone who needed it a new heart.

God has set the gift of the working of miracles in the Church as it has pleased Him. Gifts from God bless people as the Spirit wills. You have a God-given right to have the gifts of the Holy Spirit ministered to you, because God set them in the Body for its benefit. All you need to do is be there to receive them.

God's Special Gifts

God gives the ministry of the special gifts to those whom He knows He can trust. God will spiritually promote those people, if they can stand the promotions! Sometimes God decides to give a certain person a special ministry. When that happens, however, that person should stay very close to God and protect that ministry. He needs to watch himself, be obedient to God, and not think of himself more highly than he ought to think.

> For I say, through the grace given unto me, to every man that is among you, not to think of himself more highly than he ought to think; but to think soberly, according as *God hath dealt* to every man the measure of faith.
>
> For as we have many members in one body, and all members have not the same office:
>
> So we, being many, are one body in Christ, and every one members one of another.
>
> Having then gifts differing according to the grace that is given to us....
>
> **Romans 12:3-6**

At one time I participated in some meetings with Kathryn Kuhlman. She had two main gifts operating through her ministry — the gifts of healing and the word of knowledge.

Jesus had the Spirit *without* measure, but we have the Spirit of God *with* measure. If you had all the manifestations of the Holy Spirit without measure so that you could walk into a hospital and empty it of all the sick people, you would become so popular that God couldn't even put up with you. Most human beings I have known who got popular like that have fallen by the wayside or become "squirrelly." They have gone off on tangents, because they could not deal with popularity.

I always pray that God doesn't give me so much of His power that I cannot remain obedient. I pray for enough to help the people when they come to me, but not enough to make me become conceited or proud. God does give special gifts to men, but those ministries need to be protected and respected.

God's Test

God has a test for you, physically, spiritually, and financially. I pray that you will be able to pass it. Most people do not, however. You may ask, "How do I pass God's test?" Well, do you remember those high school days when you had final exams? You told your family and friends not to bother you because you needed to study all night. You had to *study* to make sure that you could pass the test.

If you don't get victory from God, you haven't passed God's test. Remember that as long as you live. And you won't pass God's test until you *make up your mind* that you are going to pass it and until you burn the midnight oil to find out for yourself what is in the Bible. You need to find out what is in the Book of Mark and what James or Peter said.

If you will learn what is in God's Word and know that you know that you know what it says, you'll pass any test that comes your way. But if you don't know what's in there, then you're not going to pass. You will always be *wondering* why, if God is supposed to be so good, He hasn't been good to you.

That is when you begin to get into all kinds of mental reasonings and false religious ideas and traditions of men trying to explain all of your own failures. You'll have excuse after excuse thinking that it may not have been God's will for you to receive something when you don't even know what is His will. But if you spend time finding out what His Word says, which is His will, then there won't be any room for doubt.

Study to Be Approved

Study to *shew* thyself approved unto God, a workman that needeth not to be ashamed, rightly dividing the word of truth.

2 Timothy 2:15

Remember that you are not studying to be approved by men, but by God. You must *show God* that you believe the Bible. But you can't believe it unless you study it and get the Word down in your spirit. God will give you the parts of the Bible that you show Him you believe. If you can't show God that you believe Him, then you won't receive anything from Him.

In Isaiah, God commands us to remind Him of His Word. Not because He is forgetful, but because he wants us to show Him that we really believe what He has told us. Then when we apply it to our lives for specific needs, He will watch over His Word to perform it.

Put me in remembrance: let us plead together: declare thou, that thou mayest be justified.

Isaiah 43:26

4

A SPECIAL MINISTRY OF FINANCES

Just as there are different gifts and callings in the Body of Christ, there are different ministries to which people are called. One of these ministries is in the area of finances or the giving of financial support.

People in this type of ministry have been given a special anointing to raise money to support the gospel of Jesus Christ. Everyone is called to give and support the work of God, but there is a special calling for some to be able to raise great amounts of money so that this gospel can be preached to all the world, and then the end can come.

A number of times God has told me that He has given me that gift and showed me how He wanted me to use it. But, remember this, God will not trust you with something unless He knows you'll be faithful to use it for Him.

One year, I was speaking at Kenneth Hagin's camp meeting in Tulsa, Oklahoma, when the Lord moved upon me with His healing power so strongly that after 30 minutes of ministering in it, I needed to be taken to my hotel room. I couldn't even stand on my own feet, so two men took me to the room. I was saturated with the power, presence, and peace of God.

The next morning when I awakened, the peace of God was still present on me just as strongly. So I sat in bed thinking about the goodness of God. All of a sudden, the wall in front of me totally disappeared, and I found myself looking into an entirely different world.

Bearing Fruit

The first thing I saw was a hill with a tree on it. Then the tree came closer, and I could see that it was a fruit tree of some kind. The tree came even closer, but the fruit had fallen off and was lying all over the ground. Then it came even closer, and this time the fruit had turned into money. *Piles* of money! The tree came even closer, and I saw that it had turned into me.

So I was lying on the bed and looking at myself with money all around the bottom of my feet — all the way up to my knees. Remember: God gives special ministries to certain people in the Church. Only God can give you a ministry. You can't get it yourself or from any man, nor can you *make* God give you a ministry. Just be faithful to Him in the ministry of helps which is for everybody.

Every ministry needs the ministry of helps functioning through it. Be faithful to God in helping people and, if God decides to use you in some other way, that is up to Him. Not being faithful hinders your promotion in the Lord. God is only going to use you and give you a ministry as His Spirit wills. He is not going to use everybody for the same thing, so don't try to make something happen in your life just because you see a gift operating in someone else's life.

Then the Word of the Lord came unto me saying, "Son, I'm calling you to — and giving to you — the ministry of *bearing fruit* for the Body of Christ. I will let you know when and how to fulfill this ministry."

Then He told me, "Tomorrow night, I want you to bear fruit for the youth group that needs a new bus. I'll let you know when." That was my first mission in this ministry of bearing fruit.

Kenneth Hagin had a youth group called the Rhema Singers who were trying to buy a bus, but didn't have enough money. That night at camp meeting, as I was sitting on the platform, the Spirit of God came upon me and let me know that it was time to *bear fruit* for the youth group. He said, "Stand up and tell them what you saw in your vision last night."

So I explained the vision and the new ministry that God had given to me. Then I said, "Now all of you who want to help these young people buy a new bus so they can go around the country presenting Jesus, get up out of your seats and pile money around my feet."

By the time all the pledges and offerings came in within a few months, the youth group had enough money to buy their bus.

The next year I was invited back to camp meeting to speak again. One morning during that week, the Lord woke me up at 6 a.m. and told me that His servant was a million dollars in debt. He said, "I'm going to give you a plan that will help you raise more than a million dollars in the offering tonight."

Then He said, "Son, if you will stick to this plan, you can tell the congregation that if they have never seen a million-dollar offering, they're about to see one."

So I stuck with the plan the Lord gave me and received the evening offering. About $1.2 million came in during that one single offering.

A few years ago, I was speaking in a meeting at Wallace and Marilyn Hickey's Happy Church in Denver, Colorado. Sunday morning, someone from the church picked me up at my motel room. As we pulled out onto the street and headed for church, the Spirit of the Lord came on me and said, "I want to use you to *bear fruit* and bless my servant Kenneth Copeland personally."

So a few days later, I was sitting in the front row at one of Kenneth Copeland's meetings. The Spirit of the Lord came upon me and said, "Now is the time when I want you to *bear fruit* for my servant Kenneth Copeland." So I got up and told Kenneth that I had to do something. I asked him what he needed. I found out that he and his family didn't have their own home. So that night, at the Lord's direction, I took up an offering for the Copelands so they could buy a new house.

Later, I was speaking in Fort Worth, Texas, for a couple of nights and the Copelands came to hear me. After the service, Kenneth came to talk to me. He asked when I was leaving, because the Lord had instructed him to fly me home personally in his private jet. He said that anyone with the kind of ministry I had needed to be treated first class.

After the service the next night, Kenneth and Gloria were driving me out to the airport where their plane was ready and waiting, and I was sitting in the back of their brand-new Mercedes.

Kenneth looked at me and said, "You know, Brother Norvel, this car cost $65,000."

I said, "No, I didn't know that."

He said, "Yeah, and I have two of them. Some people make fun of me for driving these things, but

I don't have much choice. I came home one night after a meeting, and this car was sitting in the driveway with the title to it and a note that said, 'It's a gift to you, Brother Copeland.' Someone actually gave it to me!

"It was not very long until we came home another night, and a second Mercedes was sitting there. I have two of these that were given to me. People think I used God's money to buy these cars, but I didn't buy them. They were given to me free. What am I supposed to do, Brother Norvel?"

I said, "Well, you're supposed to drive them if God gave them to you."

Then Gloria turned to me and said, "Yes, but Brother Norvel, some of the people who make fun of us for driving these cars never tell this part of the story because they don't know it. I have kept track of it and, before we received these cars, we gave away 14 cars to pastors and missionaries. Those were our own personal cars that we gave because God told us to give them. After we gave away the 14 cars, then God gave us these two first-class Mercedes, one for each of us."

Notice that they received those blessings *after* they gave away those other cars. You need to understand, however, that the blessings were for being obedient. God had told them to give those 14 cars away. They were blessed because they didn't hang on to possessions, because they put God and His Word ahead of their own convenience. If He tells you to give something away, you'd better do it. God's Word says that He wants you to prosper financially and be in good health, even as your soul prospers. It prospers your soul to be obedient to the Lord and do what He says.

As Every Joint Supplies

The Book of Ephesians tells us that the Body of
Christ operates and works together . . . **by that which**
every **joint** *supplieth,* **according to the** *effectual work-*
ing **in the measure of every part . . . .** (Eph. 4:16).

It is a vital necessity that each member in the Body
do his or her part to supply all that is needed to
accomplish the work of the gospel. It has been said that
20 percent of the people in the Church do 80 percent
of the work, and 80 percent of the people do 20 percent
of the work. According to the Bible, that is not the way
God intended for us to operate.

In a natural body, the life of that body is in the
blood. But the blood cells are formed in the marrow
of the bones. Whenever a limb of the body is *out of joint,*
it hinders the blood development and cuts off the *supply*
to the rest of the body. Even in natural things it is as
every joint supplieth, according to the effectiveness of
every part.

As a member in particular of the Body of Christ,
who has been *set* in the Church as it has pleased God,
you have a responsibility to give life or to *supply* from
what God has given you. Whether you have a *special*
ministry of giving, or whether you operate in another
area of supply such as serving, teaching, exhorting,
ruling, etc., there is a serious call to become diligent
and faithful in doing your part.

As we *show God* our commitment and diligence in
the use of the *talents* that He has placed on the inside
of us, then God can trust us with even more *respon-*
sibility. If you are not interested in using the gifts and
talents that God has given you for His work, then Jesus

considers you a . . . **wicked and slothful servant** (Matt. 25:26). Eventually He will take away your talent and give it to someone who is willing to use it for Him. I am sure that you don't want the fate of that servant Jesus was talking about to fall on you.

> **And cast ye the unprofitable servant into outer darkness: there shall be weeping and gnashing of teeth.**
>
> **Matthew 25:30**

It is time for the Body of Christ to realize that God wants each one of us to use the gifts and talents He has given us. He wants each of us to be a joint that supplies life to the Body instead of death. *No longer* can we be envious and jealous of another's gifts and talents and not willing to function in the calling God has given us.

5

HINDRANCES TO PROSPERITY

There are some vital things in a Christian's life that need to be carried out, or the blessings that come from Heaven to earth will be hindered. A major reason for the lack of blessing in Christians' lives is that they don't understand what causes the windows of Heaven to open or close.

Of course, God opens and closes them, but He doesn't open and close them just because He feels like it. There are things that He has given us to do that will cause those blessings to flow or to be cut off. Remember that God does not bless ignorance. If you're going to receive the blessings of God, you're going to have to get His wisdom. He is not ignorant, nor does He bless ignorance.

> **My people are destroyed for lack of knowledge: because thou hast rejected knowledge, I will also reject thee, that thou shalt be no priest to me: seeing thou hast forgotten the law of thy God, I will also forget thy children.**
>
> **Hosea 4:6**

Once you understand that God has put the ability for blessing or destruction in the power of our own hands, that knowledge becomes an awesome responsibility. Most Christians have been taught that God's *sovereign will* is keeping them from enjoying the blessings of His kingdom in order to keep them humble.

But the Bible says that Jesus paid the price for us to live in both *victory* and *abundance*.

> Therefore, as ye *abound* in *every thing*, in faith, and utterance, and knowledge, and in all diligence, and in your love to us, see that you abound in this grace also.
>
> I speak not by commandment, but by occasion of forwardness of others, and to prove the sincerity of your love.
>
> For ye know the grace of our Lord Jesus Christ, that, though he was *rich*, yet for *your sakes* he became poor, that ye through his poverty might be rich.
>
> **2 Corinthians 8:7-9**

Authority in Finances

God has given you all *power* and *authority* in your home and in your finances in Jesus' name. Once you are born again by the Spirit of God and become a child of God, the devil and his demons have no *right* to operate on your property, in your family, or in your finances. But you're going to have to keep the devil off your property and out of your finances, and you have to know how to do that.

> Behold, I give you power to tread on serpents and scorpions, and over all the power of the enemy: and nothing shall by any means hurt you.
>
> **Luke 10:19**

First of all, you need to get rid of the kind of thinking that asks, "I wonder if God would do that for me?" The problem always is with the receiver, not the Giver. It is a shame to have to say this, but many Christians will never receive God's abundant financial blessings, because they won't give up traditional teaching for the

50

Word of God. They may receive enough to pay their bills and a small amount left over to give or save, and that will be it.

The Holy Spirit can manifest Himself and lead you in different ways and show you how to make a million dollars. But He will never do that for most Christians. The reason that He won't is because most of them can't handle it. If they could *learn* to *obey* God and *put the gospel first*, then God said that all other things would be added unto them. If they could learn to put the gospel first — above family, above business, and above everything else — they could *have* everything else. When God said to put the gospel first, He didn't mean just to make it important — He meant *first!* That doesn't mean second.

The main reason most Christians get into trouble with God is because they want to do their own thing. When they have done all they want to do, there is no time or energy left over to pass out tracts or bring people to church. And, even if they have time, most people won't do it.

If serving Jesus is fifth or sixth down on your list of things to do, you're about as close to Him as you can get unless you change, because He is not going to change. God is not going to change, for He "changeth not." If there is any changing that's going to be done, you will have to change yourself.

God always goes by His Word that has been given us in the Bible. He does not go by anything else. He does not go by man's church services, *no matter whose they are,* unless they are based on the Bible. God has raised up churches to operate according to His Word. But, if you want to do your own thing, He will let you.

He will let you construct a building that can sit on a corner 40 years and have no cripples ever walk out healed. In fact, cripples don't walk out of most churches because there isn't enough power of the Lord in those places. There is a price to be paid to get the power of God in your life. When Jesus walked the earth, He paid the price to get that power. He prayed all night and lived in total obedience to His Father. He spoke only the Words of God, so God gave Him the Spirit without measure.

You can't go around all the time talking just any way you choose, you can't talk about other people any way you please and live any kind of lifestyle you please, you can't do your own thing and not do very much for God, and expect great blessings from Heaven to fall on you. There is only one thing that you can do to receive great blessings, and that is God's thing.

If you are not going to pay the price to get the blessings of God for your life, then you're not going to get them. You're not going to get them unless you change over to the teaching of God's Word. You must be diligent to be a good student of the scriptures.

Any cripple can get up out of his wheelchair and walk. Any blind person can receive his sight. Any deformed child can be made normal, *any of them.* But as believers we have to know how to help them do that, and unfortunately most Christians don't *know* how. So the sick and afflicted have to remain as they are.

The power of God doesn't come through newspapers, magazines, and football games. It doesn't come from tithing, teaching a Sunday school class or attending church. Dynamic spiritual power comes only through the Word of God and through fellowship with Him. You become like the people you spend time with. God is only going to trust with His power those who are like Him, not those who are like everybody else.

Put God First

If God is really first in your life, and you love Him, then you will worship Him and help spread His gospel. If you will show God that you love Him, He will bring so many blessings down from Heaven that you won't know where to put them all. But you have to *learn* to put first things first.

Master, which is the great commandment in the law?

Jesus said unto him, Thou shalt love the Lord thy God with all thy heart, and with all thy soul, and with all thy mind.

This is the first and great commandment.

Matthew 22:36-38

God said to have no other gods before Him. If you do not worship the Lord and serve and obey Him, then He is not first in your life. What you dwell on in your mind is what you serve and worship. The thing you think about habitually and continually, that is your god. You must learn to worship God *first* and make Him number one in your life.

Redeemed From the Curse

Christ hath redeemed us from the curse of the law, being made a curse for us: for it is written, Cursed is every one that hangeth on a tree:

That the blessing of Abraham might come on the Gentiles through Jesus Christ; that we might receive the promise of the Spirit through faith.

Galatians 3:13,14

The scriptures say that we are no longer under the curse of anything. So shake yourself, and get out from under anything that is a curse or is plaguing you. The price has been paid already for you to be free from it. If things don't seem to go right for you, realize that it is an attack from the devil and that you need to learn how to fight him. Rise up boldly in Jesus' name, and stop the devil and his maneuvers against you.

If, or when, the devil comes to your house trying to put back on you the curse that you've been redeemed from, if he tries to rob you of God's blessings, the first thing to say is: *"No, you don't! Not to me, you don't!"* Say it loud and clear because, in case you didn't know this, the devil is hard of hearing. You need to make him understand what you're saying because, if you don't, he won't leave. He'll do anything he wants to you.

The devil is crazy. He has lost his mind! He is possessed with himself and, at the same time, wants to be God. That is enough to make any being crazy.

Submit yourselves therefore to God. Resist the devil, and he will flee from you.

James 4:7

The devil will listen only to someone with authority. Jesus has given you that authority, if you will just make up your mind to use it. If the devil has been trying to kill you with some deadly disease or trying to steal your finances, you need to stand up boldly and run him off.

Obey Orders From Headquarters

The first part of James 4:7 says, **Submit yourselves therefore to God . . . .** That means you are going to have to obey orders from Heaven. When the Holy Spirit gives you an order, *always obey Him.* Tell God that you are always available to serve Him.

When your soul prospers in obedience to the Spirit of God, He will see to it that the blessings of Heaven will fall on you. He said that He would *open up* the windows of Heaven and pour you out a blessing. (Mal. 3:10.) *God said that He would do it.* But remember that you can't make God do anything. He pours out blessings under the conditions laid down in His Word because He watches over His Word to perform it.

> **For as many as are led by the Spirit of God, they are the sons of God.**
>
> **Romans 8:14**

Being led by the Spirit of God is the most important thing in your life. The Spirit of God promises you everything in the Bible. It is by and through the Word of God that He will manifest Himself in your life. The reason the Holy Spirit doesn't do more for you is because He doesn't agree with you. Your thinking and behavior do not line up with the scriptures.

You must receive from God by faith. That is the only way God works. Unless you put His Word on the inside of you, there is nothing in your heart for Him to be in agreement with. The Word doesn't do any good sitting on your shelf at home or kept on a cassette tape. It must be a real part of you. Unless you know what is in the Bible, God does not have anything with which to work.

One reason people in the Body don't know any more than they do about what is in the Bible is because they have not been taught. They need to be taught exactly what the Bible says, not what someone says about it or thinks it says. One thing is for certain: People are desperate for the truth in the Bible and desperate to *know* what God has said and promised to us in it.

Speak to the Mountain

And Jesus answering saith unto them, *Have faith in God.*

Mark 11:22

One of the most important decisions that you can ever make in your life is to have faith in God and to believe His Word. Then — and only then — will your life be all that God wants it to be. Unless you make up your mind to believe Him and His Word, your life will *never* be totally pleasing to Him. You'll always be living somewhere in God's permissive will. It is not His perfect will that you enjoy just a few of the things that He has promised. But it is God's will that you enjoy *everything* He has promised.

The Lord moved upon me one day to teach the Bible and to try to get His people to obey it. You see the reason most people can only enjoy the blessings of God in part is because the scriptures are not fully obeyed.

The Word of the Lord came to me saying, "I want you to start teaching the people how to *speak to mountains*. They haven't learned how to do that yet. Even though they have heard scriptures about it all their lives, they just sit there and hear it and go home and do whatever they want to do."

56

> For verily I say unto you, That whosoever shall say
> unto this mountain, Be thou removed, and be thou cast
> into the sea: and shall not doubt in his heart, but shall
> believe that those things which he saith shall come
> to pass; he shall have whatsoever he saith.

Mark 11:23

Now *whosoever* means *you!* Not someone else. And *to say* means to open up your mouth and let words and sounds come out of it. It sounds simple; but, if it really is, why aren't more people obeying this instruction? Usually, it is because their old beliefs get in the way of new revelation. But Jesus was talking to each of us. He didn't just pick out certain ones. He said *whosoever.*

Christians have heard this read to them for years, but they don't do it. They leave the church and go do whatever they feel like doing. That is why many are not receiving any more from God than they are receiving right now. As long as you flounder around and are not a good student of the scriptures and do and say whatever you please, the blessings of God are hindered from coming to you.

> But be ye doers of the word, and not hearers only,
> deceiving your own selves.

James 1:22

Being a doer of God's Word means opening up your mouth and saying something. But make certain that you always say what the Bible says, so that you are in agreement with God. Say whatever is necessary for you to be in line with the Bible.

Mountains are anything in your life that the devil brings or that are caused by the curse. It might be a disease or poverty or a temptation that would result in sin. Whatever it is, you need to speak to the mountain and do what Jesus told you to do. He said, . . . **Whosoever shall *say* unto this *mountain*, Be thou removed, and be cast into the sea . . . .**

Tell the mountain in your life to be removed and cast into the sea and you will have whatever you say, *if you don't doubt in your heart.* If you do that and remain steadfast in the faith, immovable, the mountain has no choice but to be cast into the sea. For in Matthew 21:21, Jesus said, . . . **it shall be done.**

I was teaching on this subject in a service once when a man in a wheelchair was brought to me. The Lord spoke to me and said, "What you're teaching will work for him, if he will only obey it."

So I bent down and looked at the man in the wheelchair. I told him, "Sir, the Lord spoke to me and said that if you will obey what I'm teaching here, it will work for you. I'm teaching on how to talk to your mountains, and the Lord said that if you will obey what I am teaching this morning, it will work for you.

"Talk to your mountains. Look at your crooked legs and call them straight. Talk to them because you can have what you say, if you believe in your heart and don't doubt. Call your crooked legs straight, Mister. Call your crooked legs straight. Now you do it. Call your crooked legs *straight.*"

I stood there and repeated it over and over and, at last, I bent down right next to his ear. I kept saying, "Call your crooked legs straight. Call your crooked legs straight!" I must have said that about 75 times when, all of a sudden, he came alive on the inside and said,

"I call my crooked legs straight! I call my crooked legs straight!"

He had been in that position for 25 years, and his mind believed he would be like that for the rest of his life. He never thought that God could reach out and touch him so that he could walk out of that wheelchair free. And neither would you and I, in his circumstances.

But the man said, "I call my crooked legs straight." And I said, "Thank God for that!" I had almost worn myself out trying to get him to obey the Bible and do what I was teaching. Most people could believe the Bible easier if their carnal minds did not get them in trouble. As I say to them sometimes, "Your thinker's a stinker!"

All of a sudden, the Spirit of God fell on this man in the wheelchair, and he broke and began to cry and weep. All the time that he was weeping, he kept confessing that his crooked legs were straight. As I watched him, He rose up out of his wheelchair and walked across the front of the church and all the way back again. His crooked legs had been made straight and he was able to walk normally.

When that happened, his pastor came over to me and said, "He's never been able to do anything like that before."

I said, "Of course not. He's never called his crooked legs straight before. He called them straight today, and God straightened them out and strengthened them."

The Holy Spirit is listening to every word that you say, and He is watching over the Word of God to perform it. When what you say lines up with what God says, and when you say it in faith according to Matthew 21:21 and Mark 11:23, then whatever you say will come to pass. You will have whatever you say.

6

YOU POSSESS
POWER TO PROSPER

But thou shalt remember the Lord thy God: for it is he that giveth thee power to get wealth, that he may establish his covenant which he sware unto thy fathers, as it is this day.

And it shall be, if thou do at all forget the Lord thy God, and walk after other gods, and serve them, and worship them, I testify against you this day that ye shall surely perish.

Deuteronomy 8:18,19

The Lord God tells us that we have been given the power to get wealth. But He also tells us that it is given, first of all, to establish His covenant in the earth. If you are not going to use the blessings and gifts that God gave you to spread the gospel and establish the Word of God on the earth, then God says in Deuteronomy 8:19 that . . . **ye shall surely perish.**

When God's blessings come your way, and you are enjoying being a partaker of His promises, God says that you must *remember him.* For it is *He* Who has given you the *power* to obtain that wealth. Many times, people think that they have something from God because they deserve it or because God owes them something. Well, God is under no obligation to do anything for you!

If God gave us what we deserve, we would all be in hell, paying for our sins. But it is the mercy and goodness of God that leads us to repentance. Thank God that Jesus paid the price for us and became sin for us.

> And it shall be, when the Lord thy God shall have brought thee into the land which he *sware* unto thy fathers, to Abraham, to Isaac, and to Jacob, to give thee great and *goodly* cities, which thou *buildedst* not,
>
> And houses full of all good things, which thou *filledst* not, and wells digged, which thou *diggedst* not, vineyards and olive trees, which thou *plantedst* not; when thou shalt have eaten and be full;
>
> Then beware lest thou forget the Lord, which brought thee forth out of the land of Egypt, from the house of bondage.
>
> Deuteronomy 6:10-12

I believe that God is planning on pouring out riches, honor, and blessing on many of His children. It is true that God wishes for you to be in health and prosper above all things, but there is one thing that your prosperity is not above: God Himself.

The only way God's blessings will follow you is if you make up your mind to have no other gods before Him. God says, "Beware lest thou forget the Lord thy God." He wants you to always remember to put Him first in *everything*. Not just some things, *everything*.

Power to Change Things

Included in your power to prosper is the power to change your circumstances. God has given you the power to stop anything in your life that's not of Him. You can stop a back pain, a headache, bad blood, cancer, or anything that is not from God. All you need to do is speak with authority in Jesus' name, resist whatever is coming against you, and make it stop. You may think that God's supposed to stop it, but that's not the way it works.

God does not work automatically for anybody, and He doesn't bless lazy people. He lets them die. If you are too lazy to memorize verses of Scripture and do what God has told you to do, then you're going to die. Jesus paid the price on Calvary for you to have the power and authority to control your own circumstances.

If your own natural father would die and leave you an inheritance of land or money, you would have to go and *claim* it as rightfully yours or you would never receive it. That is the same way it is with things provided for you in Christ Jesus. You just need to *learn* how to claim the things that belong to you. If I had not learned how to get and keep my freedom, I would be in bondage myself. Kick the chains of bondage off and claim your rightful freedom.

Take inventory of your life right now. If there's something in your life that you don't like, why don't you stop it? Is there a part of your life that's not the way you want it to be? Well, God has given you power and authority to speak to that thing and tell it to stop in Jesus' name. If you do that every day, it will stop.

After you have used your power and authority to stop it, you have to know how to get in agreement with the Holy Spirit so that His power can operate in your life. God will only confirm His Word with signs following. So, if you don't have scripture to cover your case, the power of the Holy Spirit will not work in your case. You can stop anything you want to stop if you have the right scripture to prove God's will and if you use the authority of Jesus' name which He gave you.

You might say that you don't know what you're going to do. Yes, you do. You're going to stay in your problems as long as you talk like that. When you don't *know* what you're going to do, I'll tell you exactly what you're going to do — *nothing*! You have to *know* what you're going to do. People who don't *know* what they're going to do aren't going to do anything. When you get tired of being in the state in which you're living, look up in the New Testament to see what God has provided for you. Then claim it boldly in the name of Jesus and take it away from the devil.

The devil is the one who stole from you in the first place. John 10:10 says that the thief has come to steal, to kill, and to destroy, but Jesus has come to give us the abundant life — the only kind of life God has for us. He is surrounded totally by prosperity and riches, and He hates all poverty, sickness, and defeat. Heaven has nothing in it but victory and abundance, and God wants His kingdom to come to His earth.

Power to Set Yourself Free

You never need to have *any* bad days, times when you are up one day and down the next, when you have victory one day and defeat the next. If there are some days when you feel like serving God and some days when you don't, you need to know that you can get victory for your life once and for all. If defeat tries to overtake you and run your life, you need to resist it. Don't accept it. Run it off.

The devil is out to destroy every day of your life, so you need to throw him out. He'll try to bring sickness, depression, and all sorts of vile things. You must resist those evils and run the devil off. Treat the devil as you would a rattlesnake, and he will go. When he sees that he can't win around you, it will be as it was when Jesus resisted him. After three times of resistance, the devil left Him to find an easier target.

> **Be sober, be vigilant; because your adversary the devil, as a roaring lion, walketh about, seeking whom he may devour:**
>
> **Whom *resist* stedfast in the faith, knowing that the same afflictions are accomplished in your brethren that are in the world.**
>
> 1 Peter 5:8,9
>
> **Put on the whole armour of God, that ye may be able to *stand* against the wiles of the devil.**
>
> **For we wrestle not against flesh and blood, but against principalities, against powers, against the rulers of the darkness of this world, against spiritual wickedness in high places.**
>
> **Wherefore *take unto you* the whole armour of God, that ye may be able to *stand* in the evil day, and having done all, to *stand*.**
>
> **Stand therefore, having your loins girt about with truth, and having on the breastplate of righteousness;**
>
> **And your feet shod with the preparation of the gospel of peace;**
>
> **Above all, taking the shield of faith, wherewith ye shall *be able* to quench *all* the fiery darts of the wicked.**
>
> Ephesians 6:11-16

When the devil comes *as* a roaring lion and shoots his fiery darts at you, *stand firm* in Jesus' name and resist the devil's lies through faith in God's Word. If the devil is trying to destroy your life in some way, say, "In Jesus' name, I resist you. *Go* from me. I take authority over every evil spirit trying to come against me, and I command you to leave and *come out of me!"*

Sometimes you need to *set yourself free.* It is wonderful when you can cast the devil out of yourself. You learn how to *shout* and say, "I'm free. Jesus set me free!" Resist the devil, then you'll always stay free. Always say what you mean. Say it *loud* and *strong* so the Lord can hear you and the devil can hear you.

Also, when something tries to attack your body or a part of your life, always check up on the amount of time you spend seeking the Lord, worshiping Him and obeying Him. *Check up on yourself,* not on someone else, check yourself! You have been given the Holy Spirit so you can know what is wrong in your life. He will show you things to come and the traps the devil has set for you down the road. I learned a long time ago that the Holy Spirit was sent here so I could live in power and victory all the days of my life.

One of the names of the Holy Spirit in John's gospel is Comforter or *parakletos,* which literally means *"one called alongside to help or aid."* It was used many times to refer to a lawyer or attorney who would stand in defense of his client. So the Holy Spirit has been sent to help or to aid us in our defense against the attacks of the devil.

> Likewise the Spirit also helpeth our infirmities: for we know not what we should pray for as we ought: but the Spirit itself maketh intercession for us with groanings which cannot be uttered.
>
> **Romans 8:26**

As you pray in the Spirit, the *parakletos* will come alongside to help strengthen your infirmities. Another word for infirmities here is *weaknesses.* That means any area of your life in which you don't have total victory. Whenever any area of your life is weak, the Holy Spirit will come and make intercession for you according to the will of God as you pray in the Spirit.

If you want to experience real *godly success* and *victory* in your life, then begin your day like this. First, worship and praise God, but do it out loud. This will bring God's presence into your life in a very real way. It also will stop and drive out those evil spirits that always are hanging around. Second, pray in the Holy Spirit, and cry out to God to come to your aid in whatever weak areas you may have. How long do you have to pray? Until you *know* that you have the victory. Of course, if you don't want victory, then don't pray at all. But the victory *belongs* to you, so you might as well get it.

When something tries to attack you, don't wait to see what is going to happen. I repeat, *don't wait.* Say *no* to the devil! Say, "I don't accept this. In Jesus' name, I command you, *go from me!*" Make that evil thing leave you. *Make* anything that is not victory depart from you!

Power to Prevail

God promises victory to us in every area of life, if we will only believe and not doubt.

For whatsoever is born of God overcometh the world: and this is the *victory* that overcometh the world, even our faith.

1 John 5:4

You can live victoriously every day of your life if you'll just take *one* verse of scripture from the Bible that covers your case, read it, and say, "It's mine. I've got it. Jesus, You sent Your Word to heal and bless me." Then quote that verse as if it belonged to you, because it does. Tell Jesus that you believe exactly what His Word says. If you'll do that and never quit, Jesus will come and bring power and victory to you every time. Don't get lazy and quit before you get the blessing.

It is hard work to get Heaven to come down to earth. Heaven doesn't come down to earth cheap! Heaven comes down to earth by *faith*. There is always a big price to pay to get Heaven's blessing down to earth. You need to know what that price is, or you will never receive the *power to prevail* that Heaven has *promised* you. Jesus said in Luke 9:24:

> **For whosoever will save his life shall lose it; but whosoever will lose his life for my sake, the same shall save it.**

The *only* way to receive all that Heaven has promised you and to be a partaker of God's *divine nature* is by not being a partaker of any other nature than His.

> **According as his divine power hath given unto us all things that pertain unto life and godliness, through the knowledge of him that hath called us to glory and virtue:**
>
> **Whereby are given unto us exceeding great and precious promises: that by these ye might be partakers of the divine nature, having escaped the corruption that is in the world through lust.**
>
> **2 Peter 1:3,4**

If you will lay down this low human nature in the form of surrender and obedience, you will receive the *divine life* of Almighty God that will enable you to live above the beggarly elements of the world. You can prevail over poverty, you can prevail over sickness and disease, you can prevail over pain and grief, you can prevail over anything that doesn't mean victory for your life. Jesus already paid the price and delegated the *power* to you. Now the choice is up to you.

Remember that every part of the gospel that you get tired of will be the part of the gospel that you never get to enjoy anymore. The reason you won't enjoy it anymore is because God won't let you have it. The easiest thing in the world for you to do is your own thing. That is why people need to know that it's real easy to go to hell. All they need do is reject Jesus, the Son of God, because they want to do their own thing, and they will be hell-bound.

Power to Perform

If you are *obedient* to do what God is telling you to do, you will receive *power* from on high. This is power to *perform* the works that God has purposed for you from the foundation of the world.

> **For we are his workmanship, created in Christ Jesus unto *good works*, which God hath before ordained that we should walk in them.**
>
> **Ephesians 2:10**

There is a divine plan or blueprint that God has ordained for your life so you can *walk in it.* That means that God has given you the *power to perform* everything He has commanded you to do. If you continue to walk in the *power* and are faithful to *perform* what God tells you to do, you will be mightily blessed the rest of your life.

69

Part of laying down your life for God is sharing His gospel with other people so they might receive of His life also. But if you aren't willing to give away to others what God has given to you, then you won't receive what He has for you either. You need to learn how to be led by the Spirit of God. If you do, then your defeated days of stupid mistakes and bad investments are all over. I learned years ago how to be led by the Holy Spirit, and I don't have any more defeated days.

No more one day up and one day down, one month up and one month down. No more making a profit one year and not making one the next. If you are led by the Spirit of God, you don't have to put up with that, and I don't.

I take victory away from the devil. He tries to steal everything. He will steal your business, your health, your children, and anything that belongs to you. Command him to go from you in Jesus' name, and do it every day until he is all gone and you're totally free.

Jesus said, **If the Son therefore shall make you free, ye shall be free indeed** (John 8:36). Jesus' words are truth. He also said, **And ye shall know the truth, and the truth shall make you free** (John 8:32). It is the knowledge of the truth that will make you free and keep you free! But you need to know the truth and *Jesus* is the *truth*. He's not anything else.

If you aren't careful, the devil will try to rob you of the blessings of God in two ways. He works through your mind and through your flesh, trying to destroy you and steal from you everything God has given you. God instructs you to keep yourself built up in the Holy Spirit so that when the tempter comes, you can resist him steadfastly in your faith, and he will flee from you. As you pray in the Holy Spirit, your own human spirit is edified, or charged up, so you can have *power to perform* — so you can be like Jesus was when He came out of the desert in the *power* of the Spirit.

Power of Patience

My brethren, count it *all* joy when you fall into divers temptations;

Knowing this, that the trying of your faith worketh patience.

But let patience have her perfect work, that ye may be perfect and entire, wanting nothing.

James 1:2-4

That ye be not slothful, but followers of them who through *faith* and *patience* inherit the promises.

Hebrews 6:12

If patience can have its perfect work in you, you won't be wanting anything because you'll have everything. Many times the reason you don't get things from God is because you don't have any patience or at least not enough patience. Faith doesn't work without patience. Faith doesn't work without love. Faith is dead without action.

If you will add patience to your faith, you will inherit the promises of God. I can tell you that I've got all kinds of faith but, if I don't have love, action and patience, there is no good going to come out of my faith.

Patience is what gets the job done. God will not answer nervous (wavering) prayers. You must have love, patience, and action, or the Bible promises won't work for you.

In order to have faith, you must have faith in something that God has promised you. You can't believe God for anything except for that which He has promised you in His Word. You can't believe God for just anything. You must have scriptures from the Bible in which God has given you His great and precious promises.

Some people want to believe God for 14 Cadillacs, and they are not even using their one Chevrolet to serve Him. God won't give you one more, if you don't use what you *already* have for Him. Show God that you're going to use what He has given you to serve Him, even if that means passing out tracts, bringing people to church, feeding the poor, and helping people. When you are faithful with the things God already has given you, then He will give you something better.

You need to be patient and faithful and keep your thinking straight in order for God to bless you. If you have a "squirrelly" mind, jumping from limb to limb all the time, God can hardly "corral" you long enough to bless you. That is the way my mind used to be all the time. So I walked the floor for three years with my hand on my head, praying. Finally, I asked the Lord to take away my carnal way of thinking and replace it with the mind of Christ. The mind of Christ is totally possessed with the God-kind of patience. Before I had the mind of Christ, I couldn't even *believe* half of the Bible.

When you pray and ask God for something, always remember, faith is not seen. If you want any kind of sight, feeling, or hearing to "prove" that you have received your request, then that's not faith, and God won't honor it.

> **Now faith is the substance of things hoped for, the evidence of things *not seen*.**
>
> **Hebrews 11:1**

If you really want to receive something from God, you must thank Him for it in advance — before you see it. If you thank Him in advance, then God will let you see it, provided you *serve* and *obey* Him. Remember that your health and prosperity from God is as your *soul* prospers. (3 John 2.)

The amount of time you spend thanking God for something, that is the amount of time the Holy Spirit works to give it to you. If you stop thanking God for it, He stops working for you. If you forget to thank God for your healing, it could cost you your life. When thanksgiving comes out of your mouth and boils up into the throne of God, and you keep on and on, finally you get the attention of God Almighty. When that happens, the *power of patience* has brought the *power of God* from Heaven down to earth.

One time, I prayed three years for the deliverance of my daughter from drugs. I kept on and on and wouldn't give up. Remember, God is not obligated to anyone no matter who you are. But if God hears faith coming up before Him, He will even use angels to deliver you if He chooses. If your faith won't waver, but is full of the *power of patience*, God will always show up.

When God looks down and sees His children thanking Him for something, His heart jumps and delights because it is God's good pleasure to give us everything He has promised us. It is God's good pleasure for us to seek Him until He manifests Himself. God does not manifest Himself to any great degree to people who do not spend time seeking Him.

If you'll be diligent to seek God and work for Him, He will manifest Himself, and you can have anything you want. You can seek God and be prosperous *in any area*. It doesn't make any difference what it is. If you seek God with all your heart, *He will cause you to prosper.*

If you will spend time seeking to know God's will so you can do it, then whatever it is, He will give it to you. You may ask, "What is God's will?" His will, for you or anybody else, is *all* of the New Testament. God will give you the part of the New Testament that you can believe.

You will never have any problems with God Almighty, Jesus, or the Holy Spirit. *All* your problems are with you and your head.

Most people are doing good if they can even find the church. This may be a shock to some people, but we are not as smart as God. He knows *exactly when* and *how* to give us things. We must keep ourselves in a position to receive what God wants us to have. This is done by continually seeking His will for our life and striving to obey His Spirit. Then we will be in good shape to receive from His hand.

You must come to a place of obedience and service, with meekness and reverence for His Word, and be able to say along with the Apostle Paul:

But what things were gain to me, those I counted loss for Christ.

Yea doubtless, and I count *all things* but loss for the excellency of the knowledge of Christ Jesus my Lord: for whom I have suffered the loss of *all* things, and do count them but dung, that I may win Christ.

Philippians 3:7,8

7

SCRIPTURE TO COVER YOUR CASE

If you are ever going to possess the victory that is rightfully yours in Christ Jesus, you will need to have scripture to cover your case. The Word of God needs to be in your heart in abundance because . . . **out of the abundance of the heart the mouth speaketh** (Matt. 12:34).

In Proverbs 4:21, we are told not to let the Word depart from our eyes but to keep it in the midst of our heart. This is essential if we want to live on this earth and prosper and have good success.

God told Joshua that the book of the law should not depart out of his mouth, but that he should meditate in it day and night so that he could *observe to do* according to all that was written therein. For then he would *make* his way prosperous, and then he would have good success. (Josh. 1:8.)

Because I know how important it is for you to have scripture to cover your case, I have included a selection of Bible promises on prosperity. If you will meditate on these verses and get them down in your spirit, then out of your heart can flow an abundance of prosperity, wisdom, and understanding.

The victory for you is *in the Word*, not somewhere else. So you need to be desperate to get God's Word

77

down in your heart. That is why I'm including the name of a tape series that has nothing but *prosperity scriptures* on it. These tapes contain hundreds of verses on the subject of prosperity, narrated in both the *King James Version* and *The Amplified Bible* translation. Because faith comes by hearing, this is the best way to get these scriptures down in your heart. I know they will bless you mightily.

The series is entitled *The Covenant of Divine Prosperity.* Just write to Covenant Cassettes, P. O. Box 734, Cleveland, TN 37311. This is a four-tape series which costs $18. If you are as desperate for God's Word as I believe you are, then these tapes need to be listened to several times a week.

Prosperity Scriptures

And he sought God in the days of Zechariah, who had understanding in the visions of God: and as long as he sought the Lord, God made him to prosper.

2 Chronicles 26:5

Beloved, I wish above all things that thou mayest prosper and be in health, even as thy soul prospereth.

For I rejoiced greatly, when the brethren came and testified of the truth that is in thee, even as thou walkest in the truth.

I have no greater joy than to hear that my children walk in truth.

3 John 2-4

A good man leaveth an inheritance to his children's children: and the wealth of the sinner is laid up for the just.

Proverbs 13:22

The eyes of all wait upon thee; and thou givest them their meat in due season.

Thou openest thine hand, and satisfiest the desire of every living thing.

Psalm 145:15,16

And they rose early in the morning, and went forth into the wilderness of Tekoa: and as they went forth, Jehoshaphat stood and said, Hear me, O Judah, and ye inhabitants of Jerusalem; Believe in the Lord your God, so shall ye be established; believe his prophets, so shall ye prosper.

2 Chronicles 20:20

Let them shout for joy, and be glad, that favour my righteous cause: yea, let them say continually, Let the Lord be magnified, which hath pleasure in the prosperity of his servant.

Psalm 35:27

Behold, God is mighty, and despiseth not any: he is mighty in strength and wisdom.

He preserveth not the life of the wicked: but giveth right to the poor.

He withdraweth not his eyes from the righteous: but with kings are they on the throne; yea, he doth establish them for ever, and they are exalted.

And if they be bound in fetters, and be holden in cords of affliction;

Then he sheweth them their work, and their transgressions that they have exceeded.

He openeth also their ear to discipline, and commandeth that they return from iniquity.

If they obey and serve him, they shall spend their days in prosperity, and their years in pleasures.

Job 36:5-11

The Lord is my shepherd; I shall not want.

He maketh me to lie down in green pastures: he leadeth me beside the still waters.

He restoreth my soul: he leadeth me in the paths of righteousness for his name's sake.

Yea, though I walk through the valley of the shadow of death, I will fear no evil: for thou art with me; thy rod and thy staff they comfort me.

Thou preparest a table before me in the presence of mine enemies: thou anointest my head with oil; my cup runneth over.

Surely goodness and mercy shall follow me all the days of my life: and I will dwell in the house of the Lord for ever.

Psalm 23

But without faith it is impossible to please him: for he that cometh to God must believe that he is, and that he is a rewarder of them that diligently seek him.

Hebrews 11:6

Only be thou strong and very courageous, that thou mayest observe to do according to all the law, which Moses my servant commanded thee: turn not from it to the right hand or to the left, that thou mayest prosper whithersoever thou goest.

This book of the law shall not depart out of thy mouth; but thou shalt meditate therein day and night, that thou mayest observe to do according to all that is written therein: for then thou shalt make thy way prosperous, and then thou shalt have good success.

Joshua 1:7,8

And keep the charge of the Lord thy God, to walk in his ways, to keep his statutes, and his commandments, and his judgments, and his testimonies, as it is written in the law of Moses, that thou mayest prosper in all that thou doest, and whithersoever thou turnest thyself.

1 Kings 2:3

The thief cometh not, but for to steal, and to kill, and to destroy: I am come that they might have life, and that they might have it more abundantly.

John 10:10

The righteous shall flourish like the palm tree: he shall grow like a cedar in Lebanon.

Those that be planted in the house of the Lord shall flourish in the courts of our God.

They shall still bring forth fruit in old age; they shall be fat and flourishing.

Psalm 92:12-14

The Lord will not suffer the soul of the righteous to famish: but he casteth away the substance of the wicked.

He becometh poor that dealeth with a slack hand: but the hand of the diligent maketh rich.

Proverbs 10:3,4

My son, let not them depart from thine eyes: keep sound wisdom and discretion:

So shall they be life unto thy soul, and grace to thy neck.

Then shalt thou walk in thy way safely, and thy foot shall not stumble.

When thou liest down, thou shalt not be afraid: yea, thou shalt lie down, and thy sleep shall be sweet.

Proverbs 3:21-24

In the house of the righteous is much treasure: but in the revenues of the wicked is trouble.

Proverbs 15:6

The soul of the sluggard desireth, and hath nothing: but the soul of the diligent shall be made fat.

Proverbs 13:4

Seest thou a man diligent in his business? he shall stand before kings; he shall not stand before mean men.

Proverbs 22:29

He that tilleth his land shall have plenty of bread: but he that followeth after vain persons shall have poverty enough.

A faithful man shall abound with blessings: but he that maketh haste to be rich shall not be innocent.

Proverbs 28:19,20

He that tilleth his land shall be satisfied with bread: but he that followeth vain persons is void of understanding.

Proverbs 12:11

If any of you lack wisdom, let him ask of God, that giveth to all men liberally, and upbraideth not; and it shall be given him.

But let him ask in faith, nothing wavering. For he that wavereth is like a wave of the sea driven with the wind and tossed.

James 1:5,6

Then shalt thou delight thyself in the Lord; and I will cause thee to ride upon the high places of the earth, and feed thee with the heritage of Jacob thy father: for the mouth of the Lord hath spoken it.

Isaiah 58:14

But of him are ye in Christ Jesus, who of God is made unto us wisdom, and righteousness, and sanctification, and redemption.

1 Corinthians 1:30

But thou shalt remember the Lord thy God: for it is he that giveth thee power to get wealth, that he may establish his covenant which he sware unto thy fathers, as it is this day.

And it shall be, if thou do at all forget the Lord thy God, and walk after other gods, and serve them, and worship them, I testify against you this day that ye shall surely perish.

Deuteronomy 8:18,19

The rich man's wealth is his strong city: the destruction of the poor is their poverty.

The blessing of the Lord, it maketh rich, and he addeth no sorrow with it.

The fear of the wicked, it shall come upon him: but the desire of the righteous shall be granted.

Proverbs 10:15,22,24

For bodily exercise profiteth little: but godliness is profitable unto all things, having promise of the life that now is, and of that which is to come.

1 Timothy 4:8

If ye be willing and obedient, ye shall eat the good of the land.

Isaiah 1:19

Do not err, my beloved brethren.

Every good gift and every perfect gift is from above, and cometh down from the Father of lights, with whom is no variableness, neither shadow of turning.

James 1:16,17

Keep therefore the words of this covenant, and do them, that ye may prosper in all that ye do.

Deuteronomy 29:9

Now, my son, the Lord be with thee; and prosper thou, and build the house of the Lord thy God, as he hath said of thee.

Only the Lord give thee wisdom and understanding, and give thee charge concerning Israel, that thou mayest keep the law of the Lord thy God.

Then shalt thou prosper, if thou takest heed to fulfil the statutes and judgments which the Lord charged Moses with concerning Israel: be strong, and of good courage; dread not, nor be dismayed.

1 Chronicles 22:11-13

Christ hath redeemed us from the curse of the law, being made a curse for us: for it is written, Cursed is every one that hangeth on a tree:

That the blessing of Abraham might come on the Gentiles through Jesus Christ; that we might receive the promise of the Spirit through faith.

Now to Abraham and his seed were the promises made. He saith not, And to seeds, as of many; but as of one. And to thy seed, which is Christ.

Galatians 3:13,14,16

And it shall come to pass, if thou shalt hearken diligently unto the voice of the Lord thy God, to observe and to do all his commandments which I command thee this day, that the Lord thy God will set thee on high above all nations of the earth:

And all these blessings shall come on thee, and over-take thee, if thou shalt hearken unto the voice of the Lord thy God.

Blessed shalt thou be in the city, and blessed shalt thou be in the field.

Blessed shall be the fruit of thy body, and the fruit of thy ground, and the fruit of thy cattle, the increase of thy kine, and the flocks of thy sheep.

Blessed shall be thy basket and thy store.

Blessed shalt thou be when thou comest in, and blessed shalt thou be when thou goest out.

The Lord shall cause thine enemies that rise up against thee to be smitten before thy face: they shall come out against thee one way, and flee before thee seven ways.

The Lord shall command the blessing upon thee in thy storehouses, and in all that thou settest thine hand unto; and he shall bless thee in the land which the Lord thy God giveth thee.

The Lord shall establish thee an holy people unto himself, as he hath sworn unto thee, if thou shalt keep the commandments of the Lord thy God, and walk in his ways.

And all people of the earth shall see that thou art called by the name of the Lord; and they shall be afraid of thee.

And the Lord shall make thee plenteous in goods, in the fruit of thy body, and in the fruit of thy cattle, and in the fruit of thy ground, in the land which the Lord sware unto thy fathers to give thee.

The Lord shall open unto thee his good treasure, the heaven to give the rain unto thy land in his season, and to bless all the work of thine hand: and thou shalt lend unto many nations, and thou shalt not borrow.

And the Lord shall make thee the head, and not the tail; and thou shalt be above only, and thou shalt not be beneath; if that thou hearken unto the commandments of the Lord thy God, which I command thee this day, to observe and to do them:

And thou shalt not go aside from any of the words which I command thee this day, to the right hand, or to the left, to go after other gods to serve them.

Deuteronomy 28:1-14

The thoughts of the diligent tend only to plenteousness; but of every one that is hasty only to want.

Proverbs 21:5

Through wisdom is an house builded; and by understanding it is established:

And by knowledge shall the chambers be filled with all precious and pleasant riches.

A wise man is strong; yea, a man of knowledge increaseth strength.

For by wise counsel thou shalt make thy war: and in multitude of counsellers there is safety.

Proverbs 24:3-6

Give, and it shall be given unto you; good measure, pressed down, and shaken together, and running over, shall men give into your bosom. For with the same measure that ye mete withal it shall be measured to you again.

Luke 6:38

By humility and the fear of the Lord are riches, and honour, and life.

Proverbs 22:4

Cast thy bread upon the waters: for thou shalt find it after many days.

Ecclesiastes 11:1

He who oppresseth the poor to increase his riches, and he that giveth to the rich, shall surely come to want.

Proverbs 22:16

Poverty and shame shall be to him that refuseth instruction: but he that regardeth reproof shall be honoured.

Proverbs 13:18

He that covereth his sins shall not prosper: but whoso confesseth and forsaketh them shall have mercy.

Proverbs 28:13

There is that scattereth, and yet increaseth; and there is that withholdeth more than is meet, but it tendeth to poverty.

The liberal soul shall be made fat: and he that watereth shall be watered also himself.

He that withholdeth corn, the people shall curse him: but blessing shall be upon the head of him that selleth it.

Proverbs 11:24-26

The rich ruleth over the poor, and the borrower is servant to the lender.

Proverbs 22:7

And Abram was very rich in cattle, in silver, and in gold.

Genesis 13:2

Moreover, brethren, we do you to wit of the grace of God bestowed on the churches of Macedonia;

How that in a great trial of affliction the abundance of their joy and their deep poverty abounded unto the riches of their liberality.

For to their power, I bear record, yea, and beyond their power they were willing of themselves;

Praying us with much intreaty that we would receive the gift, and take upon us the fellowship of the ministering to the saints.

And this they did, not as we hoped, but first gave their own selves to the Lord, and unto us by the will of God.

Insomuch that we desired Titus, that as he had begun, so he would also finish in you the same grace also.

Therefore, as ye abound in every thing, in faith, and utterance, and knowledge, and in all diligence, and in your love to us, see that ye abound in this grace also.

I speak not by commandment, but by occasion of the forwardness of others, and to prove the sincerity of your love.

For ye know the grace of our Lord Jesus Christ, that, though he was rich, yet for your sakes he became poor, that ye through his poverty might be rich.

And herein I give my advice: for this is expedient for you, who have begun before, not only to do, but also to be forward a year ago.

Now therefore perform the doing of it; that as there was a readiness to will, so there may be a performance also out of that which ye have.

For if there be first a willing mind, it is accepted according to that a man hath, and not according to that he hath not.

2 Corinthians 8:1-12

For as the rain cometh down, and the snow from heaven, and returneth not thither, but watereth the earth, and maketh it bring forth and bud, that it may give seed to the sower, and bread to the eater:

So shall my word be that goeth forth out of my mouth: it shall not return unto me void, but it shall accomplish that which I please, and it shall prosper in the thing whereto I sent it.

For ye shall go out with joy, and be led forth with peace: the mountains and the hills shall break forth before you into singing, and all the trees of the field shall clap their hands.

Instead of the thorn shall come up the fir tree, and instead of the brier shall come up the myrtle tree: and it shall be to the Lord for a name, for an everlasting sign that shall not be cut off.

Isaiah 55:10-13

Honour the Lord with thy substance, and with the firstfruits of all thine increase:

So shall thy barns be filled with plenty, and thy presses shall burst out with new wine.

Proverbs 3:9,10

He that giveth unto the poor shall not lack: but he that hideth his eyes shall have many a curse.

Proverbs 28:27

He that hath a bountiful eye shall be blessed; for he giveth of his bread to the poor.

Proverbs 22:9

In that night did God appear unto Solomon, and said unto him, Ask what I shall give thee.

And Solomon said unto God, Thou hast shewed great mercy unto David my father, and hast made me to reign in his stead.

Now, O Lord God, let thy promise unto David my father be established: for thou hast made me king over a people like the dust of the earth in multitude.

Give me now wisdom and knowledge, that I may go out and come in before this people: for who can judge this thy people, that is so great?

And God said to Solomon, Because this was in thine heart, and thou hast not asked riches, wealth, or honour, nor the life of thine enemies, neither yet hast asked long life; but hast asked wisdom and knowledge for thyself, that thou mayest judge my people, over whom I have made thee king:

Wisdom and knowledge is granted unto thee; and I will give thee riches, and wealth, and honour, such as none of the kings have had that have been before thee, neither shall there any after thee have the like.

2 Chronicles 1:7-12

Bring ye all the tithes into the storehouse, that there may be meat in mine house, and prove me now herewith, saith the Lord of hosts, if I will not open you the windows of heaven, and pour you out a blessing, that there shall not be room enough to receive it.

And I will rebuke the devourer for your sakes, and he shall not destroy the fruits of your ground; neither shall your vine cast her fruit before the time in the field, saith the Lord of hosts.

And all nations shall call you blessed: for ye shall be a delightsome land, saith the Lord of hosts.

Malachi 3:10-12

But my God shall supply all your need according to his riches in glory by Christ Jesus.

Philippians 4:19

Books by Norvel Hayes

Endued With Power

How To Live and Not Die

*The Winds of God
Bring Revival*

*God's Power Through
the Laying on of Hands*

The Blessing of Obedience

*Stand in the Gap
for Your Children*

*How To Get
Your Prayers Answered*

*Number One Way
To Fight the Devil*

*Why You Should
Speak in Tongues*

Prostitute Faith

What To Do for Healing

*How To Triumph
Over Sickness*

*Financial Dominion —
How To Take Charge
of Your Finances*

The Healing Handbook

*Rescuing Souls
From Hell —
Handbook for
Effective Soulwinning*

How To Cast Out Devils

Radical Christianity

*Secrets to Keeping
Your Faith Strong*

*Putting Your Angels
To Work*

Know Your Enemy

**Available from your local bookstore,
or by writing:**

Harrison House
P.O. Box 35035 • Tulsa, OK 74153

Norvel Hayes shares God's Word boldly and simply, with an enthusiasm that captures the heart of the hearer. He has learned through personal experience that God's Word can be effective in every area of life and that it will work for anyone who will believe it and apply it.

Norvel owns several businesses which function successfully despite the fact that he spends over half his time away from the office, ministering the Gospel throughout the country. His obedience to God and his willingness to share his faith have taken him to a variety of places. He ministers in churches, seminars, conventions, colleges, prisons — anywhere the Spirit of God leads.

For a complete list of tapes and books
by Norvel Hayes, write:
Norvel Hayes
P. O. Box 1379
Cleveland, TN 37311
*Feel free to include your prayer requests and comments
when you write.*